Contents

Comparing lengths

Point to the longest car.
Point to the widest house.
Point to the tallest tree.

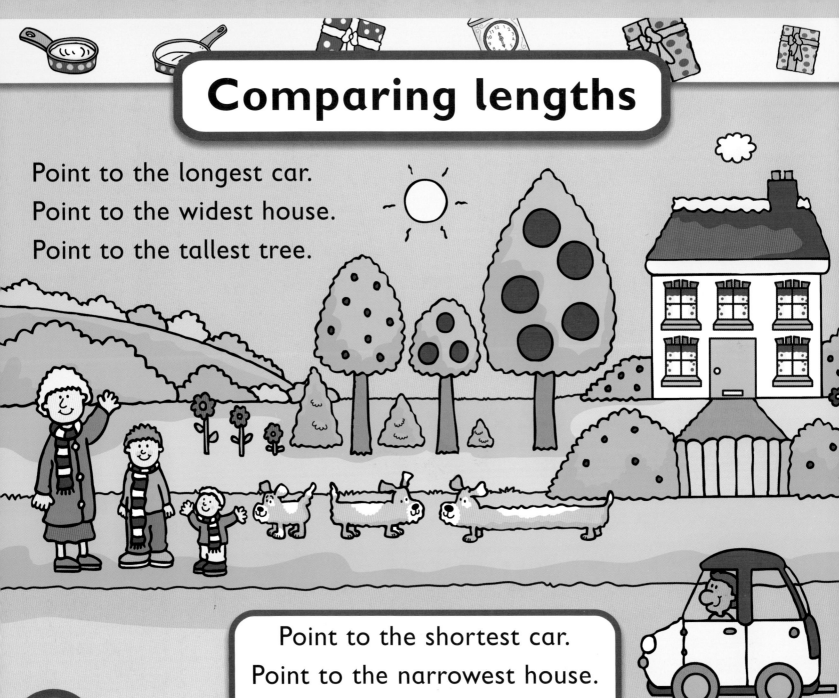

Point to the shortest car.
Point to the narrowest house.
Point to the shortest tree.

Start Maths
ON OUR WAY

Measuring

Ann Montague-Smith

QED Publishing

First published in the UK in 2004 by
QED Publishing
A Quarto Group Company
226 City Road
London, EC1V 2TT

www.qed-publishing.co.uk

A Catalogue record for this book is available from the British Library.

ISBN 1 84538 333 8

Written by Ann Montague-Smith
Designed and edited by The Complete Works
Illustrated by Jenny Tulip
Photography by Steve Lumb and Michael Wicks

Creative Director Louise Morley
Editorial Manager Jean Coppendale

Printed and bound in China

With thanks to:

Challenge

Choose 4 toys. Put them in order. Start with the narrowest. Now do this again. Start with the shortest. Is the order the same? Why do you think that is?

5

Measuring lengths

Put a strip of paper along one of the cats on page 7. Cut the strip so that it is as long as the cat. Now put the strip along the mouse ruler. How long is the cat? Measure to find the longest cat.

Which cat is the shortest?

Challenge

Use the mouse ruler to help you find toys which are about 4 mice long. Find toys which you think are shorter than 4 mice. Check with the mouse ruler.

Heaviest and lightest

Look at each balance.
Which parcel is heavier?
Which parcel is lighter?

Look at the three balances again. Can you work out which parcel is heaviest? Which is lightest?

Challenge

You need some
plasticine.
Make 3 parcels.
Guess the order
of the parcels.
Start with the lightest.
Now use a balance
to check.

How much does it hold?

Look at the pairs of containers.

Will all the water in the full container fit into the empty one?

Look at the green cup, teapot and bowl.

Which do you think will hold more than the bowl?

Which do you think will hold less than the bowl?

Challenge

Find 3 bottles of different sizes.
Decide which you think holds
least and which holds the most.
Check by filling and pouring.
Did you make a good guess?

Most and least

Which bucket do you think will hold the most sand?

Which spade do you think will hold the most sand?

Challenge

Put 4 glasses that are the same size in a line. Leave the first glass empty and fill the last one to the top with water. Then pour some water into the others so that they are in order from least to most.

13

Sequencing

Look at the pictures.

Which picture starts the story?

Tell the story in the correct order.

Down came the rain
And washed the spider out;

Incey Wincey Spider
Climbing up again.

Say the rhyme and point to the pictures in order.

Challenge

What did you do today? Tell a friend what you have done today. Start with getting up this morning.

Incey Wincey Spider
Climbing up the spout;

Out came the sunshine
And dried up all the rain;

15

Days of the week

What does Sam do on Sunday?
What does Sam do on the other days of the week?

On Monday, Sam goes to school.

On Tuesday, Sam swims with his dad.

On Sunday, Sam visits his grandparents.

On Wednesday, Sam has meatballs for tea.

Challenge

What do you do each day of the week? Draw a picture for each day of the week.

On Thursday, Sam helps to wash the car.

On Friday, Sam goes shopping.

On Saturday, Sam plays in the park.

O'clock

What is the time?

Which clock shows 5 o'clock?

Can you say all the clock times?

Challenge

You will need a clock. You say an o'clock time to a friend. Ask your friend to show this time on the clock.

I know about the words...

You will need some counters.

Listen to the words.

Put a counter on the picture that matches the words.

8 o'clock

widest

narrowest

4 o'clock

longest

shortest

tallest   **shortest**

Challenge

Find some containers. Which one is the tallest and holds most? Which one is the shortest and holds least?

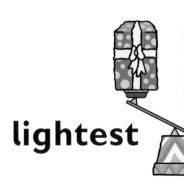

lightest   **heaviest**

holds most   **holds more**   **holds less**   **holds least**

21

Supporting notes for adults

Comparing lengths – pages 4-5

Discuss the size order of each set, such as, 'Which is the shortest tree?' 'So which tree comes next?' Use the other sets of 3 objects in the picture in the same way.

Measuring lengths – pages 6-7

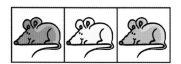

Show the children how to use the mouse ruler. Encourage the children to count the mice to find out how long each cat is.

Heaviest and lightest – pages 8-9

Begin by comparing the parcels on each balance. Now ask the children to decide which must be the heaviest and to say why they think that.

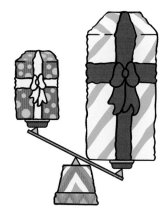

How much does it hold? – pages 10-11

Encourage the children to explain which pot they think will hold more/less. Check that they can use the vocabulary of full, empty, holds more/less…

Most and least – pages 12-13

The children are likely to have different views about which bucket or spade holds most. This activity is designed to encourage lots of talking about how much they think each one will hold, so ask the children to compare the buckets and explain their thinking.

Sequencing – pages 14-15

If the children do not know the rhyme, say it for them and ask them to point to the relevant picture each time.

Days of the week – pages 16-17

Say the days of the week together in order. Ask questions such as, 'What day is it today?' 'What day was it yesterday?' 'What day will it be tomorrow?' 'Which days do we come to school?'

O'clock – pages 18-19

If the children are unsure about o'clock times provide some clock faces and ask them to set their clocks to the times on the page.

I know about the words... – pages 20-21

Read the words under the pictures. Ask the children to say which picture shows each word. Encourage the children to show you which part of the picture depicts each idea.

Suggestions for using this book

Children will enjoy looking through the book and talking about the colourful pictures. Sit somewhere comfortable together. Please read the instructions to the children, then encourage them to take part in the activity and check whether or not they have understood what to do.

The activities encourage children to compare things for length, weight or capacity. Here it is always helpful if children make an estimate, or a guess first, then check their estimate by measuring. Ask the children to decide the order of the things, such as for length, by putting them in order from shortest to longest. Then they can make comparisons to check if they made a good guess. Estimating skills improve with practise and through checking by measuring.

In capacity, where children are filling and pouring from containers, they may need reminding that in everyday life we do not fill things to the brim. Encourage them to talk about what would happen when we tried to drink from a cup full to the brim. However, when filling and pouring, and especially when using dry sand, children will want to fill to the brim.

Children are introduced to the concept of time in this book. Encourage them to talk about things that they have done, and to put the events into order. This will help them to sequence events and to understand that something happens first, then the next thing happens… and so on. Ask questions about the days of the week, such as 'What day is it today?' 'What day will it be tomorrow… was it yesterday?' Children will begin to recognize o'clock times. Help them to link the time that the clock shows to everyday events, such as what time they get up.